BI· ·ONTAE RAS
Y RARIES)

HEINEMANN Profiles

Amelia Earhart

Sean Connolly

First published in Great Britain by Heinemann
Library, Halley Court, Jordan Hill, Oxford
OX2 8EJ, a division of Reed Educational and
Professional Publishing Ltd.
Heinemann is a registered trademark of Reed
Educational & Professional Publishing Limited.

OXFORD MELBOURNE AUCKLAND
JOHANNESBURG BLANTYRE
GABORONE IBADAN PORTSMOUTH
NH (USA) CHICAGO

Designed by Visual Image
Originated by Dot Gradations
Printed and bound in Hong Kong/China

04 03 02 01 00
10 9 8 7 6 5 4 3 2 1

ISBN 0 431 08628 1

British Library Cataloguing in Publication Data

Connolly, Sean
Amelia Earhart. – (Heinemann Profiles)
1. Earhart, Amelia, 1897-1937 – Juvenile
  literature 2. Women air pilots – United
  States – Biography – Juvenile literature
  3. Air pilots – United States –
  Biography – Juvenile Literature
I. Title
629.1'3'092
ISBN 0431086281

Acknowledgements

The Publishers would like to thank the following
for permission to reproduce photographs: Corbis:
pp4, 8, 16, 23, 24, 27, 35, 37, 38, 40, 46, 51,
National Aviation Museum pp12, 15; Hulton-
Deutsch pp26, 45, 47; Hulton Getty pp29, 30, 32,
42, 44; Purdue University Libraries: pp6, 10, 18,
20, 28, 33, 43, 49, 50, 53; Rex Features: p48.

Cover photograph reproduced with permission of
E.T. Archive

Every effort has been made to contact copyright
holders of any material reproduced in this book.
Any omissions will be rectified in subsequent
printings if notice is given to the Publisher.

For more information about Heinemann Library
books, or to order, please phone ++44 (0)1865
888066, or send a fax to ++44 (0)1865 314091.
You can visit our website at
www.heinemann.co.uk.

Any words appearing in the text in bold, **like
this**, are explained in the Glossary.

CONTENTS

WHO WAS AMELIA EARHART?

Amelia Earhart was one of the great American heroes of the twentieth century. She was born just a few years before the first aeroplane left the ground in North Carolina and, over the course of her brief life, became permanently linked with flying. Like America's other flying hero of the early twentieth century, Charles Lindbergh, Amelia Earhart seemed to **symbolize** everything that was good about her country – its willingness to take risks, the sense of fairness and decency and a 'never say die' attitude.

Amelia Earhart's face was familiar to millions of people around the world.

MYSTERY AND TRIUMPH

Unfortunately it is for Amelia's death – as much as her life – that many people remember her. She and her **navigator** Frederick Noonan disappeared in the middle of the shark-infested Pacific in 1937 as the pair were nearing the end of a round-the-world flight. The disappearance has sparked many mystery theories: books have been written and special Pacific missions launched to try to find the answer about what really happened more than sixty years ago.

What is known about Amelia Earhart, though, is the special role she played in helping the whole **aviation** industry to develop. She learned to be a pilot less than twenty years after planes were invented and went on to set – and break – many records for long-distance flights and **altitude**. She proudly hailed each triumph not so much as a personal success but as proof that women could make their mark in every walk of life.

A LASTING EXAMPLE

Amelia grew up in the rural heartland of the American Midwest and knew hard times while she was young. Her successful career, however, took her into a different world of presidents and royalty, business leaders and university heads. It is to Amelia's lasting credit that she remained much the same person throughout her life – caring and daring enough to have her 'head in the clouds'.

'I accept these rewards on behalf of the cake bakers and all of those other women who can do some things quite as important, if not more important, than flying, as well as in the name of women flying today.'

Amelia Earhart,
after being voted Outstanding American Woman of 1932.

CHILDHOOD

Amelia Earhart was born on 24 July 1897 in the small town of Atchison in the American state of Kansas. Atchison stands on the banks of the mighty Missouri River and for several decades in the mid-1800s was the last **outpost** for **pioneer** families setting off to build new lives in the American West. It is likely that in Amelia's time there were still vivid memories of those pioneering days – and of the courageous spirit of those families.

EARLY COMFORTS

Amelia spent her early years in some comfort. The Earharts had some importance in the small town.

The comfortable Earhart home reflected the family's importance in Atchison.

Millie and Pidge

Muriel, Amelia's sister, was two and a half years younger and the two children were very close. From earliest childhood they called each other by affectionate nicknames – Amelia was 'Millie' and Muriel was 'Pidge'. The two girls would spend hours reading together, imagining themselves to be explorers, horsewomen or romantic heroines.

Edwin Earhart loved to spend time with his daughters Amelia (left) and Muriel.

Amelia's father Edwin was a lawyer and her grandfather on her mother's side, Alfred Otis, was a judge. Amelia's mother Amy had been a little spoiled by the judge but she had also shown a daring streak, which Amelia **inherited**. During a trip to Colorado in 1890, Amy had become the first woman to climb Pike's Peak, a famous mountain in the Rockies.

A FATHER'S ROLE

Life in Atchsion was sometimes difficult for Amelia's father, Edwin. He felt that his **father-in-law**, Judge Otis, believed that Edwin was not good enough to marry Amy. The judge's position in the community was secure and people looked up to him, but Edwin was only a young and inexperienced lawyer. In order to prove himself to the judge, Edwin hatched a number of money-making plans that never quite worked. Once he spent many hours developing a device to hold signal flags to trains. He then

An enormous Ferris wheel was the main attraction at the 1904 World's Fair in St Louis, Missouri.

travelled the enormous distance to Washington to **patent** it, only to find that someone else had already patented a similar invention. His trip and application fee had cost a great deal of money and Edwin had to sell many of his possessions when he returned home.

Later, just when money matters were improving, Edwin spent more than $100 – a large sum in those days – to take the family to the 1904 **World's Fair** in St Louis. Amelia's grandparents thought this trip was a huge waste of money, but Amelia and Muriel had a wonderful time. Amelia had been particularly impressed by the roller-coaster at the World's Fair. When the family returned to Kansas she built a make-shift roller-coaster out of planks in the back garden. The girls' mother thought that this was too dangerous and ordered that it be taken down.

Edwin, however, enjoyed it when the girls had tomboyish fun. Both girls were extremely fond of their father. He played with them often, usually the sort of games boys would play. He took them fishing and even gave Amelia a small rifle to 'clear the barn of rats' when she was nine years old. Amelia's grandparents did not approve of this gift, which they believed was too dangerous for a child of that age – and a girl as well.

A NEW MOVE

Edwin Earhart continued to try to make life more comfortable for his family. Instead of coming up with daring plans, however, he concentrated on his work as a lawyer. One of his regular clients was a railway company, the Rock Island Line. Edwin's work on their behalf impressed the company and in 1905 they offered him a permanent job. Such a job, with its regular salary, was just what the Earharts needed, so Edwin accepted readily.

Taking the new job, however, meant that the family would have to move to the city of Des Moines in the state of Iowa, about 150 miles to the northeast. Amelia's parents went off immediately to find a new home there, leaving the little girls with their grandparents for a few weeks until the new house was arranged.

> 'Father was loving, generous but impractical.'
>
> Muriel Earhart
> in later life

A TEST OF CHARACTER

The Earhart sisters shared many interests, including dressing up and a love of animals.

The few weeks that the Earhart girls planned to spend with their grandparents turned out to be nearly a year. The girls missed their parents, who took some time finding a suitable home in Des Moines, but life in the Otis house was comfortable and their grandparents loved having them. Two of their cousins lived nearby, so they always had playmates. Although the Otises would not allow the same sort of tomboyish games that Edwin Earhart encouraged, Amelia and Muriel could play in the family orchard, barn and private park.

Amelia loved horses and became a good rider during this time. She fiddled with saddles and bridles, learning just how to make them fit comfortably on the horses and she and Muriel would even ride imaginary ponies when they were inside. The Otises encouraged reading, so the girls had a good choice of books and magazines filled with the flavour of adventure. They attended a small private school during their stay with the Otises and Amelia showed a talent for reading, writing, English, maths, French and sewing.

TOGETHER AGAIN

In 1908 Amelia and Muriel joined their parents in Des Moines. They loved being together again but missed some of the advantages of living with the Otises. At their new Des Moines home there was no orchard or park, but the girls continued with their imaginary games and their reading. *Black Beauty*, the famous story about horses, was Amelia's favourite book.

HARD TIMES

After several happy years in Des Moines, life in the Earhart household changed for the worse. Edwin began drinking heavily and finally lost his job because he was drunk so often at work. Their comfortable way of life was gone and the girls' mother had to work hard to

First impression

It was in 1908 that Amelia saw her first aeroplane. The setting was the Iowa State Fair, which was held in Des Moines. Aeroplanes were still a **novelty** but, surprisingly for someone who was to make her name as a pilot in later life, Amelia was not interested in the plane.

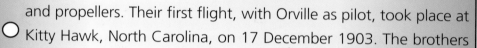

The new invention

The Wright brothers, Wilbur (1867–1912) and Orville (1871–1948) invented the first successful aeroplane. Trained as bicycle mechanics, they used their Ohio workshop to experiment with different types of wings and propellers. Their first flight, with Orville as pilot, took place at Kitty Hawk, North Carolina, on 17 December 1903. The brothers became famous overnight and toured the country with demonstrations of their plane. For many years afterwards other **pioneer** pilots demonstrated their flying skills at fairs and carnivals around the United States.

make ends meet. Amelia had never had to work before but now her sewing skills came in handy as she used old curtains to make dresses.

In 1914 Edwin was offered another job, but found that the post was filled when he arrived for work. For Amy this disappointment, coupled with Edwin's drinking, was the last straw. She decided to leave Edwin and take the girls to stay with some friends who had moved to Chicago. The three lived with their friends briefly until they found a small apartment. The girls attended Hyde Park High School and Amelia continued to study hard and get good marks. She **graduated** in 1916.

A NEW CHANCE

Meanwhile Edwin had been trying to overcome his problem with drinking. He seemed to have succeeded, so in the summer of 1916 Amy took the girls to join him in Kansas City. Amy's mother had died, leaving her some money, so she sent the girls to **private schools** to prepare them for university. Most of America's leading universities were along the East Coast – and that is where schools to prepare for university were also located. Amelia attended the Ogontz School in Pennsylvania, which was near the college of her choice, Bryn Mawr. Muriel went to a school in Toronto, Canada.

After a Christmas visit to Muriel, in early 1918 Amelia decided to leave school and move to Toronto. Canada was involved in the **First World War** and Amelia joined the war effort working as a **voluntary** nurse at the Spadina Military Hospital. In the last year of the First World War there was a terrible **epidemic** of influenza, which many of the wounded soldiers had contracted. Amelia, weakened by long hours of hard work, also contracted this illness. She had to stay in bed for several weeks and she was still recovering when the war ended on 11 November 1918. The time that Amelia spent in Toronto showed her courage and willingness to make sacrifices. It also re-introduced her to what was to become her main passion – flying.

THE 'FLYING BUG'

In the early winter of 1918 Amelia went to an airfield near Toronto to visit some of the men she had treated at the hospital. While she was there she watched the pilots practising take-offs, landings and other **manoeuvres** in small **biplanes**. Unlike her first experience with aeroplanes ten years before, when she had not been very impressed, this time she was fascinated.

Many airmen, like the pilots that Amelia watched, had learned how to fly during the **First World War**. The United States had entered the war in the last year and many Americans also became wartime pilots. After the war, these same pilots were trying to find ways of using their flying skills in peacetime. Many of them chose to earn their living by **barnstorming** – touring around the United States and Canada and showing off their flying ability.

SERIOUS ISSUES

There were other concerns for Amelia at this time. One of them was the struggle for women's right to vote. With her own tomboyish upbringing, Amelia had always felt that girls and women should have

'I remember the sting of the snow on my face when it was blown back from the propellers when the training plane took off on skis.'
Amelia Earhart, *The Fun of It*

Early biplanes looked flimsy as they edged shakily into the air.

the same chance as men to learn, work and vote for their leaders. She strongly supported the **Women's Suffrage** movement and her views are clearly shown in her letters to Muriel and her mother. Women finally gained the right to vote in the United States two years later, in 1920, and Amelia welcomed the change. This strong belief in women's **capabilities** would blossom several years later, making Amelia a household name around the world. Amelia's views were ahead of her time in this respect, since at that time many people – including many women themselves – believed that only men should have the right to vote or to hold serious jobs.

INTO THE AIR

Amelia Earhart's official Columbia University photograph shows a sense of mischief twinkling in her eyes.

I n keeping with her views on women's **potential**, Amelia enrolled in an all-female class on how to repair car engines. Her **studious** nature and natural curiosity helped her learn about the inner workings of an engine – knowledge that would help her later as a pilot.

GOING WEST

Amelia and Muriel both entered university in the autumn of 1919. Muriel went to Smith College in Massachusetts and Amelia began studying medicine at Columbia University in New York. Although she concentrated hard on her work, she also had a good deal of fun. Once she even climbed to the top of the dome of the university library and was photographed there wearing a big straw hat. By the spring of 1920, however, Amelia was receiving letters from both parents asking her to join them in California. Edwin had found a new job there, but Amy wanted Amelia's support because life was still tense between the two parents. Amelia had to leave university and cross the country to the West Coast.

The Earhart's house was large and they took in **boarders** to earn more money. One of these boarders was a young man named Sam Chapman. He came from the East Coast, so Amelia felt comfortable exploring her new surroundings with him. Their friendship deepened and the two became **engaged**. In reality, Amelia was never likely to marry Sam. He wanted a traditional wife who would stay at home – and Amelia's independent spirit would never have allowed that.

ATTRACTED AGAIN

It was not long after Amelia's arrival in California that she found herself among aircraft again. Her father took her to an air display near Los Angeles and paid ten dollars for Amelia to have a ten-minute flight. Amelia was thrilled and excited to be in the air and **resolved** to learn how to be a pilot herself. She announced this news to her family that evening. Neither parent seemed to object, so Amelia set about her plan.

'I'll see what I can do to keep Mother and Dad together, Pidge, but after that I'm going to come back here and live my own life.'

Amelia Earhart, writing to her sister before going to California

'As soon as we left the ground I knew myself I had to fly.'

Amelia Earhart, *The Fun of It*

LESSONS IN THE SKY

A melia's first flight took place at Rogers Field, situated along Wilshire Boulevard, once of the busiest roads in Los Angeles. It is hard to imagine an airfield so close to the heart of a great city nowadays, but when Amelia took her first flight aeroplanes had been around for less than two decades. The sound of whirring propellers or the sight of a **biplane** edging its way skywards brought dozens of interested spectators. Most were intrigued by the whole idea of flying, but few were daring enough to get on board an aircraft and fewer still would consider being pilots themselves. Amelia Earhart was one of those few – being a woman would put her in a very small circle of daring **aviators**.

Some years later, Amelia met up again with Frank Hawkes, with whom she made her first flight in 1920.

A DARING INSTRUCTOR

Amelia's father had agreed to her learning to fly, but he felt he couldn't afford the total cost of instruction, which was about $1000 – a great deal of money. Amelia was **persistent** and eventually Edwin decided to pay for the first few lessons. But he also made a strict condition. Edwin did not like the idea of Amelia being alone with a man in an aeroplane, so he would not allow her to take lessons from a man. Luckily for Amelia, she found out about a woman pilot nearby, who also gave flying instruction.

The pilot's name was Anita Snook, although her friends all knew her as 'Neta'. She was, if anything, even more determined to prove women's **potential** than Amelia herself.

Neta Snook

Neta had learned to fly just before the United States entered the **First World War** and had even tried to become a fighter pilot in the American armed forces. The US government would not allow women to fly, so Neta spent the war helping the British Royal Air Force look after their aircraft. And like the Canadian pilots whom Amelia had met in Toronto, Neta was determined to continue flying after the war. She bought a beaten-up Canadian plane, called a Canuck, and restored it herself. Neta took her plane across the United States, earning large sums by **barnstorming**, before setting up a flying company in Los Angeles.

AERIAL FRIENDSHIP

Amelia and Neta agreed that lessons could start. So, on 3 January 1921 Amelia arrived at the airfield dressed as she felt a pilot should be – in a full set of riding clothes. She found out, however, that for the first few weeks lessons were based on the ground, learning the basics of how planes fly, how the engine works and how to predict the weather.

It was at this stage that doubts started to arise about Amelia's **engagement** to Sam Chapman. Amelia was taking risks that Sam felt were not suited to women. Also Amelia seemed so busy working at two jobs – in a telephone office and in her father's business – to earn money for lessons, or she was spending her free time in Neta's **hangar**, getting to know more and more about planes and flying.

Neta Snook (left) was a good pilot and she became one of Amelia's closest friends.

ON HER OWN

Amelia particularly loved her lessons in the air and spent about six months learning from Neta in the two-seater Canuck. Then she became interested in buying a plane of her own. She used her earnings – and borrowed some money from her family – to buy a new plane from Bert Kinner, an **aviation engineer** who built planes in Los Angeles.

> ### An expensive hobby?
> ○ The plane cost Amelia $2000.
> ○ To pay for it, she took on jobs as a photographer and even
> ○ as a driver of a truck hauling gravel.

Amelia still needed a co-pilot, so Neta continued their lessons in the new Kinner Airstar. On 23 July 1921 Amelia and Neta were flying around Los Angeles when the plane wouldn't climb fast enough to clear a stand of trees. Amelia, at the controls, had to pull the plane up, making it **stall**. The plane plummeted to the ground nose-first. Neither woman was hurt and the plane was only slightly damaged, but it was Amelia's first crash.

Amelia was not put off flying by the experience in the slightest. In fact, not long afterwards she had her first solo flight in the Kinner and celebrated the occasion by buying herself a new leather flying coat. Now she felt herself to be a real pilot.

FLYING TO FAME

Amelia dedicated herself to flying, using every opportunity to take her Kinner plane on trips around southern California. Flying was an expensive business and most pilots found themselves struggling to find enough money to pay for fuel. Amelia was no exception and her earnings that had been used for lessons now paid for air fuel.

A RARE BREED

Amelia's friend Neta left Los Angeles at the end of 1921, leaving Amelia as the only woman pilot at her familiar airfield. She got on well with the men who worked around the airfield, putting her knowledge of car mechanics to use while learning more about how aircraft engines operated. In the small world of flying in the early 1920s Amelia became a local **celebrity**. The Los Angeles *Examiner* newspaper printed a long interview with her in 1922.

By October 1922 Amelia was confident enough to try for a flying record. Without telling them why she particularly wanted them there, she invited her family to a local airfield. Her reason became clear when she joined them in the stands later. Amelia had

'The only time a lady's name should appear in print is at her birth, her marriage and her funeral.'
Amelia Earhart's uncle, after seeing her featured in the New York Times

taken her plane up and established a women's **altitude** record of 14,000 feet (4267 m).

It was not all glory for Amelia, however. She had her share of crash-landings, with bumps and bruises to show for them. Still, this sort of adventure made Amelia even more famous, this time across the whole of the United States. Her altitude record, coupled with her daring flying, made her a familiar name to many newspaper readers. In October 1923 she was featured in a lengthy article in the *New York Times*.

Amelia's altitude record was soon broken by Ruth Nichols (centre), her friend and rival.

Concerns on the Ground

Amelia with her mother, Amy.

The following year, 1924, began with tension and unhappiness for Amelia. Her parents were not getting on and in spring they agreed to a divorce. Amy was upset by these events and Amelia felt a responsibility to help her mother. Mother and daughter agreed to travel across the country to join Muriel, who was working in Boston. Amelia sold her plane – she had bought a more advanced Kinner – and the pair took a deliberately roundabout route to reach Boston. Amelia knew that her mother would benefit from this adventure, so she made sure that the pair of them took in as much scenery and excitement as they could in the trip. By the time they arrived they had driven 7000 miles.

A social conscience

Amelia found herself in Boston with no plane and no **income**. As someone who was always busy, this meant that she had to take some sort of action. Amelia answered an advertisement and became a **social worker** in a house that looked after **immigrants** who spoke little English. She set to work with her usual enthusiasm and energy, helping the mainly Syrian and Chinese immigrants become acquainted with their new country. Amelia went far beyond her official job of teaching them English and helping the adults find jobs – she organized outings and drove her new friends around in her beaten-up car, which she called the 'yellow peril'.

A BUSINESS PROSPECT

With a new job and a regular salary coming in, Amelia was able to think about flying again. Bert Kinner contacted a Boston businessman who asked Amelia to join a project to develop a new airport near Boston. Amelia put some of her own money into the project, thereby becoming a company **director** but – more important – these new activities gave Amelia the chance to fly again.

By 1926 Amelia was in the air whenever she got the chance, flying to festivals in the Boston area and helping to **promote** not just the new airfield, but flying in general. Well-spoken and neatly turned out, she presented newspapers with the best advertisement for flying itself.

A Fateful Phone Call

Charles Lindbergh's solo flight across the Atlantic in May 1927 kept the topic of flying in the headlines for weeks on end. Lindbergh had not been the first to cross the Atlantic: other **crews** had crossed it before. Lindbergh's flight stood out because it was a solo effort. What other challenges could there be in flying across the Atlantic Ocean?

The first woman

The answer was becoming clear among those who flew: it only remained for a woman to fly across the Atlantic. By 1928 several female **aviators** began planning to do just that. One of them was Mrs Amy Guest, a rich American who lived in London. Her own family felt that the flight was too risky for Amy

Amelia with Hilton Railey.

herself and convinced her to find a replacement pilot. Mrs Guest wanted the pilot to be a well-spoken woman who would fit into English society. Hilton Railey, a friend of Mrs Guest, learned of just such a pilot. In late April 1928 he put a call through to Boston and asked to speak to Miss Amelia Earhart.

The Spirit of St Louis

In May 1927, an event occurred that took the world by storm. Until that time long-distance solo flights had all been done over land, so that pilots could make emergency landings if the weather turned bad or the plane ran into trouble. Then, on 20 May 1927 the 25-year-old Charles Lindbergh set off from an airfield near New York in the plane he called the *Spirit of St Louis*: 33 hours, 30 minutes later he had landed in Paris. The whole world hailed Lindbergh as a hero. Even after the celebrations ended on both sides of the Atlantic, Lindbergh's achievement remained a shining example of heroism and daring. The world wanted to know all about Lindbergh and publishers competed to tell his story. Such a book would sell many copies, making both Lindbergh and the publisher very rich. The man who won the **publishing rights** to tell Lindbergh's story was George Putnam, who would soon become important in Amelia Earhart's life.

THE *FRIENDSHIP* FLIGHT

Amelia Earhart and the other members of the transatlantic flight crew.

Hilton Railey asked Amelia to meet him in his Boston office to discuss a dangerous and exciting flying mission. By early May Amelia had learned of the real nature of the trip and had accepted. Mrs Guest and the other organizers were pleased with their choice, since Amelia struck them as being capable, well-spoken and attractive.

CAREFUL PLANNING

Amelia was the only woman in a three-person crew which also included experienced **aviators** Wilmer Stutz and Louis Gordon. They would fly a three-engine **amphibious** plane, called the *Friendship*, from Trepassey, Newfoundland to Europe. The flight was to take place in May, exactly a year after Lindbergh's journey. It was kept secret and Amelia did not even tell her family.

Bad weather delayed the mission, and the *Friendship* only left Boston for Newfoundland on 3 June. Two weeks later it was ready to go, but the plane would not take off under the weight of all its fuel. The **crew** dumped some of the fuel, leaving little spare, and finally took off at around noon on 17 June 1928.

ACROSS THE SEA

The news of the flight had broken in early June. Once the *Friendship* took off, the world watched and waited. The crew took the plane up until – at 10,000 feet – they were above the clouds. Amelia took her turn at the controls as the plane flew through the night.

The next morning the crew looked down and saw several ships. They discussed whether it would be safest to land there and then. They decided to carry on and about an hour and a half later, they finally saw land. They managed to land on a stretch of water near a small town. It was hard to believe that they were now on the other side of the Atlantic, less than 24 hours after taking off in Newfoundland.

After her flight Amelia described its course to eager reporters.

TOAST OF THE WORLD

The **crew** of the *Friendship* had certainly crossed the Atlantic but they had missed their expected target – Ireland – by several hundred miles. Instead they had travelled further and landed at Burry Port, South Wales.

SLOW BUILD-UP

Unlike Lindbergh's arrival in Paris in 1927, when dozens of French cars illuminated the darkened runway with their headlamps and the crowd's roar drowned out the engine noise, the *Friendship's* arrival was low-key. Several railway workers walked

Amelia enjoying her first trip, while in England, in a Moth plane.

to the waterfront, looked the plane over and returned to their work. It was nearly an hour before the first boats came out to greet the fliers and take them ashore.

The crew contacted Hilton Railey, who had sailed across the Atlantic before them and was waiting in Southampton. Within several hours he arrived with a journalist from the *New York Times*. By now the residents of Burry Port realized that they were witnessing history, and thousands of onlookers crowded round the plane and its crew.

After spending the night in South Wales, the crew woke the next morning to find a sackful of **telegrams** congratulating them. One of them, from US President Calvin Coolidge, read, 'to you the first woman successfully to **span** the North Atlantic by air the great admiration of myself and the United States'.

Singled out

It is interesting to note that the President's telegram was addressed to Amelia and made no mention of the other two crew members. Amelia was distressed by this **omission**, and the many others like it that followed. It became clear that it was her achievement – as the first woman to fly across the Atlantic – that had captured the public imagination, and Stutz and Gordon had 'gone along for the ride'.

ONE BIG PARTY

Amelia became an instant international **celebrity**. From South Wales the crew went to Southampton, where there was an even bigger reception, and then on to London. Amy Guest insisted that Amelia stay at her Park Lane house to recover from the trip, but there was a dizzying array of tea dances, dinner parties, Wimbledon tennis matches and other public functions to attend. In the midst of all the parties and interviews, however, Amelia found time to visit houses where British **social workers** carried out work similar to her own in Boston.

The **crew** of the *Friendship* finally sailed back to the United States. The reception there was even more jubilant, with huge parades in New York, Boston and Chicago.

Huge crowds lined the Southampton docks to welcome the Friendship.

THE BENEFITS OF FAME

Amelia was constantly in demand after her return to the United States. She went on lecture tours, helped

Amelia (far left) with Charles Lindberg (far right) and others in 1929.

edit major magazines and wrote a book about her adventure, entitled *20 Hrs. 40 Min.* Overseeing many of these commitments was publisher George Putnam, who had helped organize and publicize the *Friendship* journey.

Amelia's reputation was good for the **aviation** industry and in July 1929 she became assistant to the general traffic manager of Transcontinental Air Transport. But Amelia continued to fly and in August 1929 she was placed third in an all-women's air race, the Santa Monica-Cleveland Women's Air Derby. In the same year she helped the Ninety-Nines, an alternative organization for women in aviation. She seemed to have the best of all possible worlds.

'It was then that we came to realize how much water we had passed over in the *Friendship*. Eastbound the mileage had been measured in clouds, not water. There had never been adequate comprehension of the Atlantic below.'

Amelia Earhart, describing her crossing back to America

A Partner for Life

One thing that Amelia did not have during her period of international fame in the late 1920s was a husband. Amelia was not the sort of woman who needed a man to do things for her, but she had always had a romantic nature and enjoyed the idea of having someone with whom she could share her life. She was over thirty; in those days many women actively sought to be married by the time they reached that age. Seeing the troubles in her own parents' marriage had made her cautious, however. It also probably explains why Amelia didn't rush to marry Sam Chapman when they were **engaged** in California.

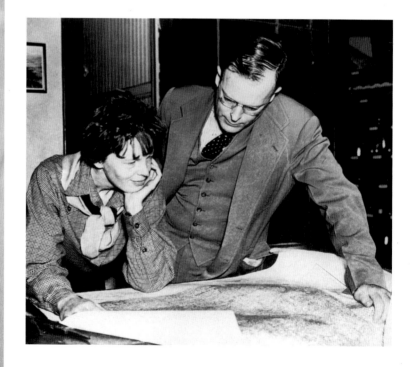

George Putnam and Amelia Earhart work on a flight plan.

Shared interests

Amelia and George were often together because of their shared business interests and also because George was as fascinated by flying as Amelia was. His pride was obvious when Amelia set a women's speed record of 181.18 mph in June 1930. He also supported her involvement with another new company, the New York, Philadelphia and Washington Airways. And it was through George's influence that Amelia's second book, *For the Fun of It*, was published in 1931.

EQUAL FOOTING

Amelia's relationship with George Putnam was very different. From the start he recognized Amelia's adventurous spirit and even encouraged it. True, George was a successful publisher and businessman, but he also enjoyed rolling up his shirtsleeves and going on long expeditions. Amelia found these qualities very attractive and their relationship deepened. George, however, was already married – although the marriage was not a happy one.

George and his wife Dorothy Binney were divorced in December 1929. Reporters soon began asking George and Amelia when they would marry. The couple kept very quiet about the matter. Then, on 7 February 1931, they married in George's mother's house in Connecticut. There were no guests and the only witnesses were George's mother, an uncle, the local judge and the judge's son.

GOING SOLO

At the time of her wedding to George Putnam in early 1931 Amelia seemed to have everything she could possibly want. She was married to the man she most loved and respected. She was famous around the world and could count Charles Lindbergh, Winston Churchill and many business leaders among her **acquaintances**. Just as important, during the terrible economic time known as the **Great Depression**, she had a large and secure fortune from all her writings, lectures and business involvement. The only thing that was lacking was the very thing that always drove her on in life – a challenge.

THE ATLANTIC AGAIN

The challenge that Amelia chose was another crossing of the Atlantic, although this time she planned to make the flight solo. The main idea behind this was a personal challenge – a chance to prove to herself that she could do it – but there were other reasons. After Amelia's triumph in 1928 some critics claimed that her involvement with that flight had been **exaggerated** and that she had merely been a passenger.

George, who took a hand in planning Amelia's career, learned that some other women **aviators** had the same idea of crossing the Atlantic alone. If any of them succeeded then Amelia's position as the world's most famous woman pilot would be challenged, leaving her in a weaker position to earn money through her fame.

SECRET PLANS

By early 1932 Amelia and George had agreed on a plan. Amelia owned a Lockheed Vega, a plane that had proved its quality and **durability** in flights up and down the East Coast of the United States. However, for a

Amelia examines her Lockheed Vega to see if it could face the transatlantic challenge.

transatlantic flight it needed to be **modified** to take a larger engine and fuel tanks. If people saw Amelia's plane being changed in this way they would know her plan. So Amelia asked her friend Bernt Balchen to 'borrow' the plane. As Balchen was planning an Arctic flight of his own, the public assumed that the work on the plane was for his journey.

The adventure begins

George had worked out the date of the flight well in advance. It was to be 20 May 1932, exactly five years after Lindbergh's heroic flight. Amelia would take off from Newfoundland again, and Balchen had the plane there by mid-May. Everything was in place for the flight and the Atlantic weather forecasts, although not ideal, suggested that they could go ahead as planned.

Amelia had one last check of the plane on the morning of the flight. Then she took a nap for several hours in the afternoon. Amelia woke, then calmly walked to the plane, started it and took off at about seven in the evening. Amelia remembered seeing a perfect sunset as she began her flight over the Atlantic.

An Irish welcome

Amelia piloted the plane skilfully throughout the flight, although she had some close calls. One of these was when she took the plane up above some thick cloud. Nearing the top of the cloud bank the plane began to feel sluggish and heavy. As Amelia realized that it was covered in ice the plane began to spin. With great presence of mind, Amelia brought the plane down to a lower **altitude** where the

AE TOOK OFF 712
NFLD PERFECT
PERFORMANCE

Telegram sent to George Putnam after Amelia's take-off

warmer air would melt the ice. Her plan worked, but Amelia could see the white caps of the ocean waves by the time the plane was back to normal.

By daylight, Amelia was relieved to see a fishing vessel below her. Land could not be far off. Eventually, to her relief, she sighted the rolling, green Irish landscape. She knew that she could not expect to find an airfield so she circled until she found a suitable pasture for her landing. At exactly 1.45 pm on 21 May 1932 she touched down near the village of Culmore in Northern Ireland.

A farm worker, who saw Amelia land, took her across some fields to the nearest farmhouse. There the owners, the Gallegher family, did what any Irish family would do for a surprise visitor – they made her a pot of tea.

The people of Culmore, Northern Ireland, were not used to American pilots landing in their fields.

FRIENDS IN HIGH PLACES

Amelia became
friendly with
Eleanor
Roosevelt, the
wife of US
President
Franklin
Roosevelt.

Amelia's reception in Europe after her flight was even more **rapturous** than after her previous triumph four years earlier. Reporters flocked to the tiny Irish village to interview her and there were many offers to fly her onwards to London. Instead, Amelia flew on a plane rented by the film company that had bought the movie rights to her story.

NATIONAL PRIDE

On the flight Amelia read some of her congratulatory **telegrams** which had come from the President of the United States, the British Prime Minister and Charles Lindbergh, among others. In London there was a whirl of social engagements.

Back in the United States, Amelia was cheered not just by the press and the public, but by important organizations. She became the first female **Honorary** Member of the National Aeronautic Association. At the White House, President Hoover awarded her a special gold medal made by the National Geographic Society – again, she was the first woman to be so honoured. The US Congress awarded her the Distinguished Flying Cross and the French government made her a member of the Legion d'Honneur.

'AE does seem to me a particularly good sport who gets all the fun there is out of what goes on, whether it be flying or gardening or fan mail.'

George Putnam, answering criticisms that women should stay at home

LIFE AT THE TOP

Later, in 1932, Franklin Roosevelt was elected President. Roosevelt was a friend of George's so there were more trips to the White House, although these visits were informal. George also had contacts in the film industry, and Amelia got to know many Hollywood stars.

The never-ending string of social and business engagements gained Amelia money and respect, but she had no time to herself for months on end. Her only regret was that she had so little time for her main interest in life – flying.

More Achievements

F̲ew people were surprised when Amelia was voted Outstanding American Woman of the Year in October 1932. She used her reputation to stress the importance of women's equality and of the need to develop the **aviation** industry.

Rewriting the record books

With the 1932 flight, in addition to being the first woman to fly the Atlantic on her own, Amelia had broken a number of records. Her flight of 2026 miles was the longest non-stop flight by a woman, her crossing had been the fastest transatlantic flight and she had become the first person to fly across the Atlantic twice. In 1933 Amelia took two hours off the Los Angeles to New York women's record, making the crossing in just over 17 hours. She then turned her attention to the Pacific Ocean.

In late 1934 Amelia conceived the idea of flying from Hawaii to California, a 2500-mile flight across the Pacific. The crossing had been made once before, but never by a solo flier. Ten pilots had already died trying to make the flight. Amelia was not

Amelia was greeted by crowds wherever she went, this time on a visit to Brussels.

outwardly concerned and plans went well for the flight on 11 January 1935. As usual, able mechanics got the Lockheed ready and George mounted a successful publicity campaign. Amelia took off on a sunny morning. The flight went exactly to plan, and Amelia touched down near San Francisco 18 hours after leaving Honolulu. Jubilant crowds welcomed her yet again.

FRIENDLY NEIGHBOURS

Amelia accepted a Mexican invitation to make a 'friendship flight' from Los Angeles to Mexico City and then on to New York. The flight began on 19 April 1935 and ended nearly three weeks later. Amelia had to wait in Mexico until the Mexican Air Force built a special runway for her plane. The landing at Newark Airport, near New York, was proof that Amelia was still a national hero – thousands thronged the runway just to glimpse the daring pilot.

'It's the first time I've ever been *asked* anywhere. I just *went* to Ireland.'
Amelia Earhart, referring to her Mexican trip

THE LAST CHALLENGE

In 1935 Amelia accepted an invitation to become part of the **faculty** of Purdue University in Indiana. She would be involved in a special department that studied careers for women. In addition, Purdue had its own airfield and a department of **aeronautics**, so Amelia saw this as a chance to combine two of the causes that meant so much to her: inspiring women to fulfil their ambitions and promoting the cause of flying.

LAYING PLANS

Amelia was planning to fly around the world from east to west, roughly along the equator. But even with the Lockheed's large fuel tanks, the long leg of the trip from Hawaii to Japan would be almost impossible. Amelia wrote straight to President Roosevelt, asking for US Navy planes to refuel her plane in mid-air over the Pacific. The President agreed, but government officials came up with a

Amelia at the controls of the Purdue Flying Laboratory.

The 'flying laboratory'

The link with Purdue also provided Amelia with the chance to buy an advanced aircraft, fitted with the most sophisticated radio and **navigational** equipment. The plane, a Lockheed Electra 10E, would be used as a 'Purdue Flying Laboratory' during Amelia's future flights, so that her flying could also work to advance **aviation** generally.

The new plane had tanks that could take it 4500 miles without refuelling. This particular item of news set people thinking. With such fuel **capacity** on her plane, Amelia could seriously consider a round-the-world flight. In fact, these guesses were accurate: Amelia had been planning just such a trip.

different solution. Amelia could use the new landing strip on tiny Howland Island.

Amelia and Frederick Noonan during the round-the-world attempt.

On 12 February 1937 Amelia and George organized a **press conference** to announce the trip. Later, on learning how difficult it would be to find Howland Island in the middle of the ocean – only two miles wide and rising to only 18 feet – Amelia invited the experienced **navigator** Frederick Noonan along for some of the journey. Also on board, for part of the trip, would be technical adviser Paul Mantz and radio operator Harry Manning.

SECOND TIME LUCKY?

On 17 March 1937 the **crew** took off from Oakland Airport in California on the first leg of the trip to Hawaii. They broke the speed record by reaching Honolulu in less than 16 hours but had to wait 24 hours before continuing because of weather

The crash landing in Hawaii was a serious setback to Amelia's flight plans.

conditions. Then, at sunrise on 20 March, they had a crisis. Just as the plane was building up speed to take off it began to swerve and then turned almost round. The landing gear was crushed and rescuers rushed to save the crew in case of fire. Many experienced pilots blamed Amelia for not steering properly.

After two months the plane was ready for a second attempt, this time heading east. On 21 May Amelia left Oakland with Frederick Noonan; George Putnam and the Lockheed mechanic Bo McKneeley went as far as Miami. Then, on 1 June, Amelia and Noonan set off for Puerto Rico and then Africa. They crossed Africa and Arabia, then called at Karachi and Calcutta, where they landed on 17 June. Then they continued through Thailand, Singapore and Indonesia. On 29 June they arrived at Lae, Papua New Guinea.

RADIO SILENCE

On 2 July Amelia and Noonan set off from Lae for the most difficult leg of the journey – to the airfield on tiny Howland Island. There were regular radio reports with Lae for the first six or seven hours, then Amelia kept in contact with American ships in the area. Eighteen hours into the flight she reported that they were 'a hundred miles out' from Howland. The airfield prepared for her arrival but in her next message Amelia reported that they were running low on fuel and couldn't see the island. At 20.14 hours GMT the USS *Itasca* received its last message from Amelia's plane. And then there was silence.

'KHAQQ to Itasca. We are on the line of position one five seven dash three three seven. Will repeat this message on 6210 kilocycles. We are running north to south.'
    Amelia Earhart's last radio message, using her code letters KHAQQ

Amelia's plane passed over one of America's most famous landmarks – the Golden Gate Bridge – shortly after take-off on her first round-the-world attempt.

A Lingering Legacy

It was impossible to believe that America's most beloved pilot could have gone missing and yet that was the truth that faced George Putnam as he paced up and down the US coast guard headquarters in San Francisco. He was joined by Frederick Noonan's wife Bea and the pair anxiously awaited any sort of news from the Pacific. It was a helpless period for George, who could do nothing apart from insist that the Navy make every effort to find the lost plane.

The US Navy, meanwhile, had sent several ships, including an aircraft carrier, to search the area around Howland Island. Over the next five days American naval ships, in particular the battleship *Colorado*, explored the region. Three **reconnaissance** planes from the *Colorado* searched from the air, trying to scan every island and even **reef** where Amelia and Noonan might have found shelter. Only one island in the search area was **inhabited**, but the people who lived there had not heard of Amelia or seen anything unusual. Overall, more than 25,000 square miles were covered in this search.

Howland Island was a tiny target to reach amid the vastness of the Pacific Ocean.

WORLD
FLIGHT

Amelia
Earhart

WORLD
FLIGHT

Amelia Earhart

HARCOURT, BRACE
AND COMPANY

For many people, Amelia's legacy lies in her clear accounts of her daring flights.

British and Japanese ships joined the search and it was estimated that more than 4000 seamen from different nations were involved. More than a quarter of a million square miles had been scoured before the search was officially abandoned on 18 July. George had to agree that his wife had died.

THE EARHART MYSTERY

The public loves a mystery and the disappearance of Amelia Earhart remains one of the most intriguing of the twentieth century. Most people accept that the plane was probably blown off course on its way to tiny Howland Island and that it crashed and sank in the open water. That region of the central Pacific has many sharks, so Amelia and Frederick Noonan would probably not have survived long in the water.

Letters from the grave

In the days after Amelia's disappearance, George had an unexpectedly sad task. In the weeks after her disappearance many letters from Amelia arrived; they had been written as part of a diary and sent from different airfields during her journey. It was difficult for George to receive these, but being a professional publisher he collected them and had them printed as a book entitled *Last Flight*.

Others have come up with different theories about Amelia's flight and her disappearance. The Pacific was the scene of fierce fighting in the **Second World War**, and some people believe that Amelia was actually spying for the United States in the years before the war. They believe that she was captured in Japanese territory and taken prisoner. In 1944 US Marines landing on the Pacific island of Saipan claimed to have found a photo album of Amelia. George Putnam made a special trip there, but he found no trace of Amelia and none of the islanders knew about her.

Amelia, shown here with film stars Cary Grant and Myma Loy, was a huge star in her own time.

TYING UP LOOSE ENDS

More recently there have been efforts to solve the mystery of Amelia's disappearance and to finish the work she started. The Earhart Project, begun in 1988, sent out teams to the Pacific to use scientific methods to discover the answer. They believe that Amelia and Frederick Noonan crashed at the **uninhabited** Nikumaroro island group. A mission in 2000 aims to provide definite evidence.

In 1997 the American pilot Linda Finch re-created Amelia's last flight in a Lockheed Electra like the one in which Amelia and Frederick Noonan had flown. Her successful flight was entitled World Flight 1997. The date of her flight would have been Amelia's hundredth birthday.

More important than the wealth of theories about Amelia's disappearance is the **legacy** that she has left. It is true that her last trip was never completed, but in some ways it is also appropriate. Through her example, she had opened the door for other women. It would be wrong to say that Amelia Earhart single-handedly caused the social advances that led to greater equality between men and women, but her life was an example of high achievement when there were many obstacles to overcome.

Amy Johnson was another female aviator who completed many long-distance flights. Her plane disappeared over the North Sea in 1939.

'I want to do it because I want to do it. Women must try to do things as men have tried. When they fail their failure must be but a challenge to others.'
Amelia Earhart, writing to George Putnam

AMELIA EARHART – TIMELINE

1897	Born in Atchison, Kansas (24 July)
1904	Visits **World's Fair** in St Louis, Missouri
1905	Stays with sister Muriel at grandparents for one year while parents find new home in Iowa
1914	Moves, with mother and sister, to Chicago
1916	**Graduates** from Hyde Park High School, Chicago
1918	Becomes **voluntary** nurse in Toronto, Canada
1919	Enrolls at Columbia University, New York
1920	Leaves university to join parents in California
1921	Has first flying instruction near Los Angeles
1922	Sets women's **altitude** record
1923	Featured in long story in the *New York Times*
1924	Finds a job as a **social worker** in Boston
1928	Becomes first woman to fly across the Atlantic Ocean; writes the book *20 Hrs. 40 Min*
1929	Appointed assistant to the general traffic manager of Transcontinental Air Transport; placed third in Santa Monica to Cleveland Women's Air Derby
1930	Sets women's speed record of 181.18 miles per hour; serves as vice president for public relations of the New York, Philadelphia and Washington Airways
1931	Marries publisher George Putnam
1932	Becomes first woman to make solo flight across the Atlantic. Voted Outstanding American Woman of the year
1935	Completes first solo flight over Pacific from Hawaii to California; makes first solo flight from Los Angeles to Mexico City; accepts post as 'visiting **faculty** member' at Purdue University
1937	Disappears over the Pacific near the end of a round-the-world flight with **navigator** Frederick Noonan

GLOSSARY

acquaintances people someone knows, but not as closely as friends

aeronautics the science of flight

altitude height, especially of an aircraft

amphibious for an aircraft, able to land on land and water

aviation flying in man-made aircraft

aviation engineer someone who studies the machinery used in powered aircraft

aviator a pilot of a man-made aircraft

barnstorming displaying flying skills to a paying audience

biplane an aircraft with two pairs of wings, one over the other

boarder someone who rents a room in a house and often has meals there

capabilities the overall ability of people to do things

capacity in an aircraft, the amount of fuel a plane can hold

celebrity someone who has become very famous

client someone who pays for the services of another person such as a lawyer

crew the pilot, mechanic and other members of a team who fly together

director someone with the power to make decisions for a company

durability ability to stand up to a great deal of wear and tear

edit to prepare a piece of writing so that it can be published

engaged having promised to marry someone and made the news public

engagement the public news that two people will be married

epidemic a widespread outbreak of a serious disease

exaggerate to go beyond the truth in describing something

faculty the teachers and instructors at a college or university

father-in-law the father of someone's wife or husband

First World War a war (1914–18) between Germany, Austria and their supporters against Britain, France, the United States and their supporters

graduate to complete one's schooling and receive a certificate, or someone who has done so

Great Depression a period (1929–39) of great poverty and hardship around the world

hangar a large building in which aircraft are stored

honorary receiving a title because of being respected

immigrant someone who moves permanently in a country to start a new life there

income a regular supply of money to provide a way of paying for living expenses

inhabited having people living there

inherit to get money or property when a relative or friend dies, or to be born with a characteristic that comes from a parent or relative

legacy what is remembered about someone after he or she dies

manoeuvres special drills and practice motions by a ship, or plane to test the skill of the pilot or the performance of the vehicle

modified improved by adding or replacing certain parts

navigational having to do with steering or planning a course of a vehicle

navigator the person who decides the course a vehicle will take

novelty something that is new and unusual

omission something that is left out, often by mistake

outpost a location that is very remote

patent the legal right to produce something, which also denies others the same right

persistent being very determined and making many efforts to achieve something

pioneer someone who goes to a new area to clear the land, build a home and start a new life

potential the overall ability of a person

press conference a public meeting where people answer questions from reporters

private school a school at which parents, rather than the local authority, pay for the education of the children

promote to talk about something publicly in order to make it more well known

publishing rights the legal right to print something, which others cannot print

rapturous excited and very pleased

reconnaissance finding information by travelling around and reporting

reef a series of rocks near the surface of the ocean, which sometimes jut out and form small islands

resolved made a promise to oneself

Second World War a war (1939–45) between Germany, Japan and their supporters against Great Britain, the United States, the Soviet Union and their supporters

social worker someone who helps poor or needy people to fit into society

span stretch from one side to the other

stall the condition of an aircraft that has lost the air speed necessary to move forward, and when it seems to briefly hang motionless in the air

studious working hard on all types of schoolwork

symbolize to be an excellent and typical example of something

telegram a type-written message sent by wire, usually as short as possible

uninhabited having no one living there

voluntary helping out without receiving any pay

Women's Suffrage the idea that women should have the same right to vote as men

World's Fair A large fair that usually includes pavilions featuring the accomplishments of individual countries or international companies

INDEX